Legal Essentials

Data Protection

Hammond Suddards Edge

Chartered Institute of Personnel and Development

Design and typesetting by Beacon GDT, Ruardean, Gloucestershire.
Printed in Great Britain by the Cromwell Press, Trowbridge, Wiltshire.

British Library Cataloguing in Publication Data
A catalogue record for this book is available from the British Library

ISBN 0 85292 861 0

The views expressed in the book are the authors' own and may not necessarily
reflect those of the CIPD. Although the CIPD has made every effort to ensure
that the information in this book is both accurate and up to date, the Institute
accepts no responsibility for any errors or omissions. It should be noted that
ultimately only the courts can interpret the law. The law in this book is stated as
at May 2000.

Chartered Institute of Personnel and Development
CIPD House, Camp Road, London SW19 4UX
Telephone 020 8971 9000 Facsimile 020 8263 3333

E-mail: cipd@cipd.co.uk Website: www.cipd.co.uk

Incorporated by Royal Charter. Registered charity no. 1079797

Contents

The authors

Hammond Suddards Edge run the popular legal advisory service for CIPD members, which takes literally thousands of calls a month from practitioners worried about the legal implications of their job. Most of those calls are concerned with the issues covered by this series. Judith Firth, legal adviser on the CIPD legal advisory service, and Hammond Suddards Edge partner and Head of Employment Unit Susan Nickson write from extensive experience in the area of employment law. Judith will also be familiar to readers of *People Management* magazine for her regular column on employment law issues.

Statutory Instruments made under the Data Protection Act 1998

Data Protection (Conditions under Paragraph 3 of Part 2 of Schedule 1) Order 2000

Data Protection (Corporate Finance Exemption) Order 2000

Data Protection (Crown Appointments) Order 2000

Data Protection (Designated Codes of Practice) Order 2000

Data Protection (Fees under Section 19(7)) Regulations 2000

Data Protection (Functions of Designated Authority) Order 2000

Data Protection (International Co-operation) Order 2000

Data Protection (Miscellaneous Subject Access Exemptions) Order 2000

Data Protection (Notification and Notification Fees) Regulations 2000

Data Protection (Processing of Sensitive Personal Data) Order 2000

Data Protection (Subject Access) (Fees and Miscellaneous Provisions) Regulations 2000

Data Protection (Subject Access Modification) (Education) Order 2000

Data Protection (Subject Access Modification) (Health) Order 2000

Data Protection (Subject Access Modification) (Social Work) Order 2000

Data Protection Tribunal (Enforcement Appeals) Rules 2000

Data Protection Tribunal (National Security Appeals) Rules 2000

Frequently asked questions

What data is covered by the Act?

Data covered by the Act is information:

- being processed by means of equipment operating automatically in response to instructions given for that purpose, eg information stored in a computer

- recorded as part of a relevant filing system

- which forms part of an accessible record.

Personal data is data which relates to living individuals who can be identified from the data. Sensitive personal data is any personal data consisting of information relating to:

- racial or ethnic origin

- political opinions

- religious beliefs or beliefs of a similar nature

- membership of a trade union

- physical or mental health or condition

- sex life

- the commission or alleged commission of any offence or any proceedings relating to the commission or alleged commission of any offence.

Who is covered by the Act?

The Act not only relates to employers and employees, but also applies to almost anyone who processes or stores personal data and to the subjects of that information. Outside the UK, the Act will only apply where the employer is established in the UK and is processing data for the purposes of that establishment or where the employer is not established in the UK or the EEA but uses equipment in the UK for processing data. 'Being established in the UK' is defined in section 5(3) of the Act as referring to:

- an individual who is ordinarily resident in the UK

- a body incorporated under the law of the UK

- a partnership formed under the law of the UK

- anyone else who maintains an office, branch, agency or regular practice in the UK.

When does the new Act apply?

The new Act came into force in the UK on 1 March 2000. However, many employers will not have to comply with all of the provisions of the Act until 24 October 2001 (if the transitional provisions apply to them).

The first transitional period is from 24 October 1998 to 23 October 2001. During this period, manual data is exempt from the data protection principles, the rights of employees under part 2 of the Act and the notification provisions. Automated data processed by reference to an individual (which will cover most data) is exempt from any of the provisions of the Data Protection Act 1998 (DPA 1998) that were not originally in the DPA 1984.

The second transitional period is from 24 October 2001 to 23 October 2007. This transitional period only applies to manual data held immediately before 24 October 1998 and manual health records that do not form part of a relevant filing system. The second transitional period gives exemption to the first five data protection principles and to the employee's right to go to court for an order requiring the employer to rectify, block, erase or destroy inaccurate data.

What is the significance of sensitive personal data?

Restrictions are imposed on the processing of sensitive personal data by the new Act. The main issue for employers is that the employee must give explicit consent to the processing of this type of data. There is no definition of explicit consent in the Act, but it is likely to mean that the consent must relate to the processing of specific sensitive personal data rather than general blanket consent.

How will the Act affect employers asking questions on application forms relating to sensitive personal data?

Employers will need to consider carefully the questions they ask on application forms that would need the consent of the prospective employee. An exception to the requirement for consent is where the information consists of data regarding racial or ethnic origin and is necessary for the purpose of monitoring equality of opportunity or treatment. Otherwise, other than some general exceptions, the consent of the applicant would be required (see 'Sample consent form' on page *x*). Where a job applicant submits a CV that consists of sensitive personal data, this act is likely to amount to explicit consent.

Will an employee have the right to see a reference given by their employer?

No. An employee does not have the right to access a reference given by their employer for the purposes of employment of the employee (although the employee could apply to their new employer for a copy of the reference). The employee may access a reference given by a third party (eg a former employer), although this would disclose the party's identity and so consent may need to be obtained.

What security measures should an employer put in place?

As part of the notification process, employers will need to advise the Data Protection Commissioner of the security procedures they intend to put in place. Employers will need to consider the reliability of employees who have access to employee records and other personal data and, where external companies are used, ensure that appropriate security measures are in place and that they are followed.

What is notification?

The new system of notification replaces the old system of registration under the DPA 1984. Certain data in the DPA 1998 cannot be processed without an entry in the register that contains the identity of the data controller.

When does an employer have to notify?

If a data controller is already registered under the DPA 1984, they do not have to notify under the new Act until the expiry of their existing register entry or 23 October 2001, whichever is the earlier. This does not mean that a data controller is exempt from other parts of the legislation, such as the data protection principles, until the above date.

What happens if an employer breaches the terms of the DPA 1998?

The Commissioner has powers to enforce the provisions of the Act. Under the DPA 1998, the Commissioner can ask the employee for specified information to ascertain whether a breach has occurred and, if one has, can ask the employer to take remedial steps. The Commissioner may also apply for a warrant to enter and inspect premises where there are reasonable grounds for suspecting that an offence under the Act has been committed.

An employee who has suffered damage as a result of a breach of the Act may claim compensation at the High Court or a county court, including claims for any distress suffered.

Sample consent form

Below is an example of a two-part form covering both personal data and sensitive personal data. A company may use this form to obtain the consent of employees to use such data about them, in accordance with the terms of the Data Protection Act 1998. The form is for illustrative purposes only and may require 'tailoring' to the needs of a specific employer and its workforce.

THE DATA PROTECTION ACT 1998: AN EXPLANATION

The Data Protection Act 1998 regulates the use of information about an individual and requires that any person, firm or company (called the 'data controller') who is to use information about an individual does so in accordance with the data protection principles.

The Act also introduces safeguards in relation to 'sensitive personal data', which includes information on:

- ethnic or racial origin

- political opinions

- religious beliefs or other beliefs of a similar nature

- membership of a trade union

- physical or mental health

- sex life

- criminal offences, criminal proceedings and convictions.

The Act requires that before a data controller can process personal data – and, in particular, sensitive personal data – the individual who is the subject of the data must give his or her express consent to the use of the information.

You therefore have the right to refuse to give your consent to the processing of such information, if you so indicate on the attached consent form.

CONSENT FORM (FOR PERSONAL DATA)

The Data Protection Act 1998 regulates the use of information about an individual and requires that any person, firm or company who is to use information about an individual first obtains the consent of the individual.

.... [the Company] will use the information you give in this form to assess your eligibility for employment provided you have first given your consent. Please sign below as appropriate.

I consent/do not consent to the processing of personal data.

Signed .... Date ....

CONSENT FORM (FOR SENSITIVE PERSONAL DATA)

To: .... [the Company]

I have read an explanation of the Data Protection Act 1998 provided to me by [*insert name*].

I expressly *consent/do not consent to [the Company] processing personal data during my employment and, in particular, sensitive personal data, in accordance with the provisions of the Data Protection Act 1998.

Signed .... Date ....

*Delete as appropriate

Introduction

With the Data Protection Act 1984 (DPA 1984) having been in force for well over a decade, why do we need more legislation now? In simple terms, the answer is that legislation was required to implement the EU Data Protection Directive (No 95/46) into UK law. The Directive dealt with the protection of individuals with regard to the processing of personal data and the free movement of such data. The Directive dealt with a wider range of issues than that covered by our domestic law and controversially applied to the processing of manual data as well as computerised data.

The new Data Protection Act 1998 (DPA 1998) received Royal Assent on 16 July 1998 and came into force on 1 March 2000, becoming fully effective after 23 October 2007 (see Chapter 5). The 1998 Act strengthens and extends the data protection regime created by the 1984 Act and applies to anyone (not just employers and employees) who processes, stores or is the subject of personal data. A number of new statutory instruments have been passed dealing with subordinate legislation (see page *v*). In particular, the new Act:

- restates the data protection principles

- applies to certain structured manual records

- introduces conditions for the processing of personal data

- introduces additional conditions for the processing of sensitive personal data

- renames the Data Protection Registrar as the Data Protection Commissioner and strengthens the Commissioner's powers

- introduces new notification rights

- introduces new rights as to the transfer of data to countries outside the EU.

The office of the Data Protection Commissioner has published guidance as to implementation of the new Act and announced its intention to publish a Code of Practice under the DPA 1998 to give details of good practice to employers. The Commissioner will also have dual responsibility for other freedom of information issues (see Chapter 6).

The purpose of this guide is to provide a summary of the new legislation with practical examples for employers. It includes a reminder of some of the key features of the existing legislation, an overview of the structure of the new legislation and the likely implications for employers. Most employers, however small, now use computers to store data and information about their employees and prospective employees, and to comply with the requirements of new legislation in relation to record-keeping (eg the Working Time Regulations 1998). It is essential that they understand the application of the new legislation – and the risks of failing to comply.

Definitions in the Data Protection Act 1998

Data – Personal data – Sensitive personal data – Processing – Relevant filing system – Accessible record – Data controller and data subject – Data processor – Third party – Recipient

To understand the provisions of the DPA 1998, it is essential to identify the meaning of various terms used. The purpose of this chapter is to provide an explanation of the key terms, some of them common to the DPA 1984. The provisions are contained in section 1 of the Act.

DATA

'Data' is information which:

1. is being processed by means of equipment operating in response to instructions given for that purpose

2. is recorded with the intention that it should be so processed

3. is recorded as part of a 'relevant filing system' (see below)

4. does not fall within the above but forms part of an accessible record.

Points 1 and 2 relate to automated data and point 3 to manual data. Point 4 is a residual category. Although the definition of data and automated systems is similar to the definition in the DPA 1984, it has been extended to cover all types of computer equipment, such as laptops, organisers and palm pilots, as well as other types of equipment, such as audio and video systems and telephone logging/surveillance systems.

PERSONAL DATA

Personal data relates to a living individual who can be identified:

- from the data

- from the data and other information in the possession of, or likely to come into the possession of, the data controller.

Personal data also includes any expression of opinion about the individual and any indications of the intentions of the data controller or any other person in respect of the individual (the latter was previously excluded by the DPA 1984). Additionally, if data is held and elsewhere in the organisation a code book is kept that helps unlock that data, both would be covered by the provisions of the DPA 1998. There is some personal data that employees are not entitled to see, such as references (see Chapter 4 for more information).

SENSITIVE PERSONAL DATA

Sensitive personal data is data as to the data subject's:

- racial or ethnic origin
- political opinions
- religious beliefs or other beliefs of a similar nature
- membership of a trade union
- physical or mental health or condition
- sex life
- criminal offences
- criminal proceedings and convictions.

For further information on criminal convictions and their disclosure, see Chapter 3.

PROCESSING

Processing means obtaining, recording or holding the information or data, or carrying out any operation or set of operations on the information or data, including:

- organisation, adaptation or alteration
- retrieval, consultation or use
- disclosure by transmission, dissemination or otherwise making available
- alignment, combination, blocking, erasure or destruction.

This is a far wider meaning than that which applied under the DPA 1984. Processing could include organising, adapting, altering or retrieving data or information contained in the data. Word processing is no longer excluded, although mere text preparation is. *Just about any activity involving data, it appears, is covered by the DPA 1998*, eg sending e-mail, opening and reading a manual file or looking at data on screen.

RELEVANT FILING SYSTEM

A 'relevant filing system' is any set of information relating to individuals to the extent that, although the information is not automatically processed, the set is structured either by reference to individuals or by reference to criteria relating to individuals in such a way that specific information relating to a particular individual is readily accessible.

The definition does not apply to miscellaneous collections of paper about individuals (even if the collections are assembled in a file with the individual name or other unique identifier on the front) if specific data about the individual cannot be readily extracted from the data collection. Notes made by a line manager on an ad hoc basis that are not stored within a filing system are unlikely to be covered.

Clearly, although there is not yet any case law, the new legislation seeks to include the vast majority of filing systems under the definition of 'relevant filing systems'. Structural card systems, for example, will count, as will a personnel file on a named individual if this is indexed and specific papers are flagged. E-mails too will almost certainly be found to be a 'relevant filing system', because it is possible to search and sort them as well as put them in chronological order.

For further developments on freedom of information and unstructured information held by public authorities, see Chapter 6.

ACCESSIBLE RECORD

An 'accessible record' is:

- a health record (information relating to physical or mental health made by or on behalf of a health professional in connection with the care of the individual)

- an educational record (records relating to pupils at a school processed by the governing body or a teacher as defined in schedule 11)

- an accessible public record (housing and social services records, as defined in schedule 12).

DATA CONTROLLER AND DATA SUBJECT

A 'data controller' is a person who (alone, jointly or in common with other persons) determines the purposes for which and the manner in which any personal data is (or is to be) processed. A data controller includes companies, businesses, organisations (such as trade unions) and local and central government. Most employers who keep records relating to staff and job applicants will be data controllers.

A 'data subject' is an individual who is the subject of personal data and may be a job applicant as well as an employee.

DATA PROCESSOR

A 'data processor' is any person (other than an employee of the data controller) who processes the data on behalf of the data controller (eg an agency or contractor).

THIRD PARTY

A 'third party' is any person other than the data subject, the data controller, any data processor or other person who is authorised to process data for the data controller or processor, eg a payroll company.

RECIPIENT

A 'recipient':

- is any person to whom the data is disclosed, including any person (such as an employee or agent of the data controller, a data processor or an employee or agent of a data processor) to whom the data is disclosed in the course of processing

- does not include any person to whom disclosure is or may be made as a result of, or with a view to, a particular enquiry made in the exercise of any power conferred by law.

2 The data protection principles

The first principle – *What is consent?* – The second principle – The third principle – The fourth principle – The fifth principle – The sixth principle – The seventh principle – The eighth principle

The DPA 1998 is built around eight data protection principles that apply to all personal data processed by data controllers. These principles are broadly similar to those contained in the DPA 1984. The principles are set out in schedule 1 of the DPA 1998 and apply to all employers. Schedules 2, 3 and 4 provide further conditions for dealing with the data. The purpose of this chapter is to provide a summary of the meaning and application of each principle. There are transitional provisions applicable, which are set out in Chapter 5. The transitional provisions provide relief from the requirements of the DPA 1998 that are over and above those that were required by the DPA 1984 (see Chapter 5 for details on transitional relief). Broadly, the principles state that personal data shall:

- be obtained and processed fairly and lawfully

- be held only for lawful purposes, which are described in the register entry

- be used or disclosed only for lawful or compatible purposes

- be adequate, relevant and not excessive in relation to the purpose for which they are held

- be accurate and, where necessary, kept up to date

- be held no longer than is necessary for the purpose for which they are held

- be accessible to individuals it concerns, who may, where appropriate, correct or erase it

- be surrounded by proper security.

THE FIRST PRINCIPLE

Personal data shall be processed fairly and lawfully and, in particular, shall not be processed unless:

- *one of the conditions in schedule 2 is met*

- *in the case of sensitive personal data, at least one of the conditions in schedule 3 is also met.*

The conditions contained in schedule 2, at least one of which must be met, are:

- the consent of the data subject has been obtained

- the processing is necessary for the performance of a contract with the data subject

- the processing is necessary for compliance with a legal obligation to which the data controller is subject (eg PAYE/NI contributions)

- the processing is necessary to protect the vital interests of the data subject

- the processing is necessary to carry out public functions and for the administration of justice

- the processing is necessary to pursue the legitimate interests of the data controller, or of a third party, or of parties to whom the data is disclosed, unless prejudicial to the interests of the data subject.

At least one of the conditions contained in schedule 3 must also be met for the processing of sensitive personal data (in addition to the requirements under schedule 2), namely:

- the explicit consent of the data subject must have been given

- the processing is necessary to comply with an obligation or legal duty imposed on the data controller

- the processing is necessary to protect the vital interests of the data subject or another person (this may only be claimed where the processing is necessary for matters of life and death, eg disclosure of a data subject's medical history to a hospital casualty department treating the data subject after a road accident)

- the processing is carried out by certain non-profit bodies

- the information contained in the personal data has been made public by the data subject

- the processing is necessary for, or in connection with, legal proceedings (including prospective legal proceedings)

- the processing is necessary for the purpose of exercising legal rights or obtaining legal advice

- the processing is necessary to carry out public functions or for the administration of justice

- the processing is necessary for medical purposes, such as preventive medicine and diagnostic research (carried out by a health professional)

- the processing is necessary for equal opportunities monitoring.

Clearly the new restrictions on the processing of sensitive personal data are likely to apply to data on job applicants and will have implications for questions asked on job application forms and at interview. Accordingly, if an employer wants to ask questions on an application form or at an interview concerning, for example, an individual's health or trade union membership, the employer should first obtain the applicant's explicit consent to the use of such information (eg by including with the application form a consent form together with an explanation of the Act and requiring the job applicant to complete and return the consent form). (See 'Sample consent form' on page *x*.)

An employer who is asked for a reference by a third party on one of its existing employees must ensure that it has obtained the employee's explicit consent where the reference includes information relating to the employee's health, criminal record or other 'sensitive personal data' as defined in Chapter 1.

What is consent?

One of the conditions for fair processing is that it is carried out with the consent of the data subject. Consent is not defined in the DPA 1998. For the processing of sensitive personal data, the consent must be explicit (see above); this is likely to require the employee to take some form of positive action, such as signing a form. For other data (ie not sensitive personal data), 'less explicit' consent is required, such as a term incorporated into a contract of employment. Employers would be well advised to consider what kind of information they ask their employees to provide and for what purposes that information is likely to be used. This may also include developing a clear policy as to the details that should be included in personnel records. For example, is it necessary to ask employees to provide details of their marital status (personal data)? Does an employer need to record on an employee's personnel file that they are HIV-positive (sensitive personal data)?

In deciding whether data has been processed fairly, schedule 1 part 2 provides that consideration must be given to the basis on which data is obtained. Data is to be treated as fairly obtained when obtained from a person authorised or required by law to provide it. The data will not be treated as processed fairly unless the data controller ensures, so far as is practicable, that the data subject has, is provided with or has made available to him or her, at least:

- the identity of the data controller (or any nominated representative, eg the employer)

- the purposes for which data will be processed (eg salary review, promotion)

- any further information necessary.

This is known as the fair processing code. This may also have a bearing on the validity of any consent given by the data subject to the processing.

THE SECOND PRINCIPLE

Personal data shall be obtained only for one or more specified and lawful purposes, and shall not be further processed in any manner incompatible with that purpose or those purposes.

The purpose of obtaining the data may be specified in a notice given in accordance with the fair processing requirements or in a notification (see Chapter 5 for more information on notification). In deciding whether a disclosure is compatible, consideration must be given to the purposes for which the data is to be processed by the person to whom it is disclosed.

Registration of the purposes for obtaining data will not give automatic compatibility with the DPA 1998. Under the DPA 1984, someone who was exempt from registration was exempt from compliance with the Act. Under the DPA 1998, that link has gone. Every data controller has to comply with the Act even if he or she is exempt from notification.

THE THIRD PRINCIPLE

Personal data shall be adequate, relevant and not excessive in relation to the purpose or purposes for which it is processed.

This is the same as under the DPA 1984. The personnel files of long-serving employees may contain a backlog of out-of-date or irrelevant information. Employers should review their personnel files periodically to ensure that there is a sound business reason to continue to hold the information and that excessive information is not held on an employee without justification.

THE FOURTH PRINCIPLE

Personal data shall be accurate and, where necessary, kept up to date.

This is more onerous than the DPA 1984 because employers have to take steps to ensure accuracy. However, this principle will not be contravened, even if data is inaccurate, where it accurately records information obtained from the data subject or a third party in any case where:

- the data controller has taken reasonable steps in the circumstances to ensure accuracy

- if the data subject has challenged the accuracy of the data, the data indicates this.

Employers may find it easier to achieve compliance with this principle by providing employees with a copy of their personnel files at regular intervals and to set up a procedure by which employees can raise queries and notify any changes to the information stored.

THE FIFTH PRINCIPLE

Personal data processed for any purpose or purposes shall not be kept for longer than is necessary for that purpose or those purposes.

The minimum period of time for which an employer will wish to keep a record is until the risk of potential legal action has passed (eg for an action of personal injury, three years). Employers may keep basic information for longer periods of time to produce references.

THE SIXTH PRINCIPLE

Personal data shall be processed in accordance with the rights of data subjects under this Act.

A person will contravene this principle only if he or she:

- fails to properly respond to a subject access request

- fails to respond to notices from individuals exercising their rights to prevent processing where the processing is

  - likely to cause damage or distress (section 10)

  - for direct marketing (section 11)

  - in relation to automatic decision-taking (section 12).

For further details, see Chapter 3.

THE SEVENTH PRINCIPLE

Appropriate technical and organisational measures shall be taken against unauthorised or unlawful processing of personal data and against accidental loss or destruction of, or damage to, personal data.

The measures in place must ensure a level of security appropriate to the nature of the data and the harm that might result from a breach of security. The data controller must take reasonable steps to ensure the reliability of any employees who have access to the personal data.

The data controller must:

- choose data processors who provide sufficient guarantees in respect of security measures they adopt

- take reasonable steps to ensure compliance with those measures

- ensure that the processor has a written contract requiring him or her to act only on instructions from the data controller and to take appropriate security measures.

Employers using computer systems should adopt necessary back-up procedures so that data is not lost as a result of system malfunctions. Additionally, only particular authorised persons should have access to the employee data. In assessing whether appropriate security exists, the data controller should consider:

- the nature of the personal data and the harm that would result from a breach of security

- access to the place where the personal data is stored, together with precautions against hazards such as fire

- measures taken for ensuring the reliability of staff who have access to the data

- formulating a policy so that

  - personal data can only be accessed, altered, disclosed or destroyed by authorised staff

  - authorised staff act only within the scope of their authority

  - should the data be accidentally lost or destroyed, it can be recovered so as to prevent any damage or distress from being caused to the data subjects.

THE EIGHTH PRINCIPLE

Personal data shall not be transferred to a country or territory outside the European Economic Area, unless that country or territory ensures an adequate level of protection for the rights and freedoms of data subjects in relation to the processing of personal data.

In determining whether there is an adequate level of protection, the following shall be taken into consideration:

- nature of personal data

- country of origin of information

- country of final destination

- purposes and period of processing

- law in foreign country

- international obligations of foreign country

- enforceable codes of conduct or one-off arrangements

- security measures.

Circumstances where the eighth principle does not apply to a transfer of personal data are set out in schedule 4:

- the data subject has given consent to the transfer

- it is necessary for the performance of a contract between the data controller and the data subject

- it is necessary for a contract with a third party

- there is substantial public interest

- it is for the purpose of, or in connection with, legal proceedings, legal advice or legal rights

- it is for the protection of the vital interests of the data subject

- the transfer is part of the personal data on a public register

- the transfer is made on terms which are of a kind approved by the Commissioner

- the transfer has been authorised by the Commissioner.

This principle did not appear in the DPA 1984. In practice an exception will often apply, eg where the transfer is necessary for the performance of an employment contract.

There are a number of exemptions that apply to some or all of the data protection principles. For more information, see Chapter 4. If an employer contravenes any of the principles, the Commissioner may issue an enforcement notice. See Chapter 5 for more details.

Individual rights

Right of subject access – Enforced subject access – *Criminal convictions – Health records* – Individual's right to access health records – Processing likely to cause damage or distress – Right to prevent processing for purposes of direct marketing – Rights in relation to automated decision-making – Rectification, blocking, erasure and destruction – Assessment

The purpose of this chapter is to give a brief summary of an individual's rights under part 2 of the new Act. The subject access provisions under the DPA 1984 have been enhanced. The new Act states that individuals have certain rights in respect of data held about them by another party. The rights are:

- the right of subject access

- the right to prevent processing likely to cause damage or distress

- the right to prevent processing for the purposes of direct marketing

- rights in relation to automated decision-taking

- the right to take action for compensation if an individual suffers damage through any contravention of the Act by the data controller

- the right to take action to block, rectify, erase or destroy inaccurate data.

RIGHT OF SUBJECT ACCESS

Under section 7 of the DPA 1998, (on application in writing and on the payment of a fee) an individual may request from the data controller:

- to be told whether personal data about him or her is being processed

- to be given a description of the data concerned, the purposes for which it is being processed and the recipients or classes of recipient to whom it is or may be disclosed

- to have communicated in an intelligible form the personal data concerned and any information available to the data controller as to the source of the data

- to be informed in certain circumstances of the logic involved in computer-assisted decision-making.

The data controller must deal with a request for subject access within 40 days of receipt of the request. These provisions mean, in effect, that employees may request to see data either in a computer or on paper that is held about them. In relation to paper-based records it will mean supplying a paper copy, and in relation to computerised records it could mean supplying a copy via e-mail. Any documents that are not intelligible must be explained. Since personal data includes any expression of opinion about an individual, if the employer has made any adverse comments (eg on the personnel file) in relation to performance, the individual has a right to see them.

An employer does not have to supply information unless he or she has received a written request and a fee of not more than £10 (Data Protection (Subject Access) (Fees and Miscellaneous Provisions) Regulations 2000).

For information on references and other individual issues, see Chapter 4.

The Data Protection Commissioner (formerly Registrar) has also announced that a draft Code of Practice governing the issues of personal data and use of employee records is to be circulated for consultation with representatives of employers and employees (see Chapter 6 for more details).

ENFORCED SUBJECT ACCESS

Criminal convictions

The problem of enforced subject access, where data subjects are forced to obtain access to their information to provide it to third parties (such as prospective employers) is also addressed by the DPA 1998 under section 56. This section makes it an offence to require an individual to provide a record obtained by virtue of that individual's right of access, where the information is required in connection with employment, or the provision of services, and where the information would reveal prior conviction or caution details. This could mean that an employer could not make a job offer conditional upon a candidate's providing it with details of convictions.

This particular provision will not apply until sections 112, 113 and 115 of the Police Act 1997 come into force, which will give the employer direct access to criminal records. This Act establishes a system of certificates that contain information about criminal convictions and that may be requested by employers.

Health records

Under section 57 of the DPA 1998, an individual may also not be forced to supply or produce a health record that has been obtained under the subject access provisions. Any contractual term that requires an individual to do this is void (see below).

INDIVIDUAL'S RIGHT TO ACCESS HEALTH RECORDS

The definition of data may also include health records if the data forms part of an accessible record and so is subject to individual access rights under the Act. A health record, made by a health professional responsible for the care of a particular individual, may relate to his or her physical or mental health or condition. This information will also amount to sensitive personal data. However, where access to this information would cause serious harm to the physical or mental health of an employee, the information may be withheld as long as the employer has consulted with a health professional. The provisions of the DPA 1998 do not affect the provisions of the Access to Medical Reports Act 1988.

PROCESSING LIKELY TO CAUSE DAMAGE OR DISTRESS

Under section 10 of the DPA 1998, an individual has the right to issue a notice requiring his or her employer not to process personal data where processing is likely to cause damage or distress him or her or a third party. The data controller must reply within 21 days, stating that he or she has complied or intends to comply, or why the notice or any part of it is regarded as unjustifiable.

RIGHT TO PREVENT PROCESSING FOR PURPOSES OF DIRECT MARKETING

By written notice, an individual may require the data controller to cease or not to begin processing personal data relating to him or her for the purposes of direct marketing. This is defined as the communication (by whatever means) of any advertising or marketing material that is directed to particular individuals.

RIGHTS IN RELATION TO AUTOMATED DECISION-MAKING

Under section 12, an individual is entitled by written notice to require the data controller to ensure that no decision *that significantly affects* him or her is based *solely* on the processing by automatic means of personal data of which that individual is the data subject.

Where a data controller has taken such a decision based solely on automated processing, the data controller must, as soon as is reasonably practicable, notify the individual.

Initially this was perceived to be an important issue for employers and human resource specialists. However, in practice, section 12 should not present too many problems because it only applies to decisions that are based *solely* on automatic processing. This is only likely to have an impact in relation to recruitment. However, employees do have a right not to have significant decisions made about them based solely on the results of automatic processing, eg psychometric testing or CV scanning. The data controller must, as soon as is reasonably practicable, notify the individual concerned of the automated process.

The individual is entitled, by notice in writing within 21 days to the data controller, to require the data controller to reconsider the decision or to take a new decision otherwise than on that basis – the 'data subject notice'.

There are exceptions to section 12. An automated decision is exempt from these provisions if it is taken for the purpose of:

- considering whether to enter into a contract with the data subject

- entering into or performing such a contract

- complying with a condition authorised or required by law.

Section 12 will not apply to a decision in relation to the above points if:

- the effect of the decision is to grant a request of the data subject (eg a holiday request granted by automated means only)

- steps have been taken to safeguard the interests of the data subject (eg by allowing representation).

These provisions might apply in the employment arena, eg where applicants complete a standard application form or aptitude test that was subject to a preliminary computerised scan. An applicant rejected at this stage with no right of review could serve a data subject notice asking for the decision to be reconsidered. On the other hand, if the employer provided some right of review against that decision in any event, then there would be no need for the candidate to receive a separate notification.

In the event of a failure to comply with section 12, the employee may apply to the High Court or a county court for an order to force the employer to reconsider its decision or take a fresh decision based on non-automated means.

RECTIFICATION, BLOCKING, ERASURE AND DESTRUCTION

An individual may apply to a court to order a data controller to rectify, block, erase or destroy personal data of which the individual is the data subject if:

- the data is inaccurate

- the individual has suffered damage because of a contravention of the DPA 1998 by the data controller and there is a substantial risk of further contravention.

If the court makes such an order, it may also order the data controller to notify third parties to whom the data has been disclosed of the rectification, blocking, erasure or destruction. In determining whether this is reasonably practicable, the court shall have regard in particular to the number of persons who would have to be notified. This section will also be applied to personal data that contains an expression of opinion that appears to be based on the inaccurate data.

ASSESSMENT

Any person may ask the Commissioner to assess whether or not it is likely that any processing of personal data has been or is being carried out in compliance with the DPA 1998. This may subsequently lead to the Commissioner's taking enforcement action (see Chapter 5).

Exemptions

National security – Crime and taxation – Health, education and social work – Regulatory activity – Special purposes – Research purposes – Information required to be made public – Disclosures required by law – Domestic purposes – Miscellaneous exemptions – *Confidential references given by the data controller – Management forecasts/ planning – Negotiations – Legal professional privilege*

The purpose of this chapter is to examine the exemptions available to certain provisions of the DPA 1998. There are a number of exemptions to the DPA 1998 that are provided in sections 28 to 36 and schedule 7. Below is a brief summary.

NATIONAL SECURITY

If required for the purposes of national security, personal data is effectively exempt from the DPA 1998's provisions, including subject access, notification and the data protection principles.

CRIME AND TAXATION

Personal data processed for one of these purposes is largely exempt from the first data protection principle and from subject access to the extent to which the application of these provisions would be likely to prejudice the purpose of the processing.

This covers data processed for:

- the prevention and detection of crime

- the apprehension or prosecution of offenders

- the assessment or collection of any tax or duty or of any imposition of a similar nature.

Employers as well as the police and other government departments can rely on this exemption.

HEALTH, EDUCATION AND SOCIAL WORK

Section 30 provides that the Secretary of State may exempt or modify the obligation to inform individuals of the purposes for which their data will be processed and the right to subject access. In the case of data processed for carrying out social work, the Secretary of State shall confer exemption or modification only where he or she considers that not to do so would be likely to prejudice this work. This category covers personal data:

- relating to the physical or mental health or condition of the data subject

- relating to present or past pupils of a school where the data controller is a proprietor or teacher

- processed by government departments, local authorities or voluntary organisations in the course of or for the purposes of carrying out social work in relation to the data subject or other individuals.

REGULATORY ACTIVITY

Section 31 provides an exemption from the obligation to inform individuals of the purposes for which their data will be processed and the right to subject access to the extent that the proper discharge of such regulatory functions would otherwise be likely to be prejudiced. This category covers the processing of personal data by public watchdogs concerned with the protection of members of the public, charities or fair competition in business.

SPECIAL PURPOSES

Personal data processed for journalistic, artistic or literary purposes is exempt from various provisions, including the data protection principles (except the seventh) and subject access where the data controller reasonably believes that compliance is incompatible with these special purposes. This exemption is to ensure the right to freedom of speech.

RESEARCH PURPOSES

Where personal data processed for research, statistical or historical purposes does not support decisions affecting particular individuals is not likely to cause substantial damage or distress to any data subject, such processing does not breach the second principle and the data may be retained indefinitely, despite the fifth principle. As long as the results of the research are not published in a form that identifies any data subject, there is no right of subject access to the data.

INFORMATION REQUIRED TO BE MADE PUBLIC

Personal data consisting of information the data controller is legally required to make public is exempt from:

- subject access and the obligation to inform data subjects of the purposes

- the fourth principle (data must be accurate and up to date) and the court's power to require rectification or erasure

- any constraints on disclosure.

DISCLOSURES REQUIRED BY LAW

Personal data may be disclosed and will not be in breach of the non-disclosure provisions where it is made available:

- as required by law, including a court order

- in connection with any legal proceedings

- for obtaining legal advice

- to establish, exercise or defend legal rights.

However, such data is not exempt from the subject access provisions unless it can be argued that it falls within the legal professional privilege exemption (see below).

DOMESTIC PURPOSES

Personal data processed by an individual only for the purposes of that individual's personal, family or household affairs (including recreational interests) are exempt from:

- the data protection principles

- part 2 (individual rights)

- part 3 (notification requirements).

MISCELLANEOUS EXEMPTIONS

These exemptions are mainly in relation to the subject access provisions. Those of relevance in the employment field are as follows.

Confidential references given by the data controller

Confidential references given or to be given by the employer for the purposes of education, training, employment, appointment to office or the provision of any service are exempt from the subject access provisions. Accordingly, it would appear that employees will not be able to gain access to copies of personal references given by their current employers. However, the exemption does not appear to cover references received by the current employer or references given by a third party, eg a former employer, that are held in an employee's current personnel file.

That said, where a subject access request is made for such a reference and complying with that request would result in the disclosure of another individual's identity (usually the author of the reference), there is no obligation to disclose that reference unless the individual who can be identified has consented to the disclosure, or it is reasonable to comply with the request notwithstanding the lack of consent. However, even where complete disclosure is not possible, an employer should still give as much of the information requested as can be given without disclosing the identity of information sources by, for example, omitting names.

Management forecasts/planning

Personal data processed for the purposes of management forecasting or planning are exempt from the subject access provisions if disclosure would prejudice the conduct of the business. This would potentially cover data processed in connection with proposed redundancies, company takeovers or employees' long-term career prospects, and would allow the company to plan such matters on a confidential basis.

Negotiations

Personal data consisting of records of the employer's intentions in relation to negotiations with the employee are exempt from the subject access provisions if disclosure would be likely to prejudice those negotiations. This would potentially cover records of negotiations in connection with pay increases, promotion or severance packages.

Legal professional privilege

Personal data consisting of information in respect of which a claim to legal professional privilege could be maintained in legal proceedings are exempt from the subject access provisions, ie a confidential communication between the employer and its legal adviser. (See also 'Enforced Subject Access' in Chapter 3.)

Transitional provisions, notification and enforcement

Transitional provisions – *General transitional arrangements* –
Transitional arrangements: automated data – *Transitional
arrangements: manual data* – *Transitional arrangements:
notification* – *Transitional arrangements: Commissioner's powers* –
Transitional arrangements: complaints and assessments –
Enforcement – *Enforcement notice* – *De-registration notice* –
Transfer prohibition notice – Offences under the DPA 1998
– Notification – Compensation

The purpose of this chapter is to identify the transitional provisions in
force, to outline the rules on notification and to identify the means of
enforcing the DPA 1998.

TRANSITIONAL PROVISIONS

General transitional arrangements

All the provisions of the new Act will not have to be complied with
straight away. Transitional relief is contained in schedule 8 for all or part
of the DPA 1998 and is available only for eligible data. This is personal
data subject to processing that was already under way immediately before
24 October 1998 and forming part of a relevant filing system. The periods
during which transitional relief is available are:

- automated data – until 23 October 2001

- manual data – until 23 October 2007.

Therefore data controllers who began processing personal data for the
first time after 24 October 1998 will have to comply with the new
legislation. From an employer's point of view, one of the interesting
areas that this impacts on is references. Where a prospective employer
that was in existence prior to 24 October 1998 receives a reference, the
prospective employee is unable to gain access to that reference. Although

initially it may appear that the processing was not under way prior to 24 October 1998, the view may be taken that recruitment is an ongoing process for an organisation, which therefore falls within the transitional relief.

Transitional arrangements: automated data

Eligible automated data is exempt until 23 October 2001 from those provisions of the DPA 1998 that were not also provisions of the DPA 1984, namely:

- the conditions for legitimacy of processing

- the restrictions on processing sensitive personal data

- the restrictions on transfer of data outside the EEA

- the additional subject access and compensation rights

- the rights relating to the prevention of processing

- the rights related to automated decision-making

- the requirements for a data processor to be bound by contract to maintain appropriate security.

Certain exemptions in the DPA 1984 are preserved until 23 October 2001, namely:

- automated data processed for a specified list of payroll and accounts purposes

- processing by an unincorporated club on its members

- processing of mailing lists

- back-up data produced to cover the loss, destruction or impairment of other data.

Transitional arrangements: manual data

Processing of manual data held in a relevant filing system will be exempt from the data protection principles, part 2 (data subject rights) and part 3 (notification requirements) of the DPA 1998 until 23 October 2001.

The following exemption also applies in relation to manual data until 23 October 2007. Manual data that was held immediately before 24 October 1998 is exempt from:

- the first data protection principle (that data shall be processed fairly and lawfully), except for the fair processing code requiring information to be provided to the data subject

- the second principle (that personal data shall only be obtained for specified and lawful purposes), third principle (personal data shall be adequate, relevant and not excessive), fourth principle (personal data shall be accurate and kept up to date) and fifth principle (personal data shall not be kept for longer than is necessary)

- an individual's request for a court order requiring his or her employer to rectify, block, erase or destroy inaccurate data held on him or her.

Transitional arrangements: notification

A data controller who is registered under the DPA 1984 on the date the notification requirements under the DPA 1998 came into effect is exempt from notification until the expiry of the existing registration or until 24 October 2001, whichever is the earlier.

Transitional arrangements: Commissioner's powers

The Data Protection Registrar has been renamed the Data Protection Commissioner. At a more substantive level:

- the effect of an enforcement notice or a transfer prohibition notice under the DPA 1984 is preserved to the extent to which the matters it deals with are enforceable under the DPA 1998 (see 'Enforcement' below)

- enforcement notices can be issued under the DPA 1998 for contraventions prior to commencement of the new Act.

Transitional arrangements: complaints and assessments

- Complaints received before the commencement date of the DPA 1998 are dealt with under the DPA 1984 provisions.

- Requests for assessment received after the commencement date are dealt with under the DPA 1998 procedures.

- In either case, the procedures can take account of whichever of the old and new principles and provisions were applicable to the processing.

ENFORCEMENT

The 1998 Act places duties on the Commissioner to promote good practice and publicise information about data protection and the law.

The Commissioner is entitled to serve enforcement notices upon a data controller who the Commissioner is satisfied has contravened or is contravening any of the data protection principles. The notice will require the data controller to take or refrain from taking specified steps or to refrain from processing personal data altogether. Failure to comply with the notice is an offence. The Commissioner may make an assessment as to whether or not it is likely that processing has been or is being carried out in compliance with the provisions of the DPA 1998. To this end, the Commissioner may serve an information notice on a data controller requiring the data controller to provide information relating to compliance with the data protection principles.

This may also extend to special information notices where the data controller claims that the special purposes exemption applies and the Commissioner suspects that the personal data is not being processed only for the special purposes, or that the data is being processed with a view to the publication by any person of any journalistic, literary or artistic material that has not been previously published by the data controller.

The extensive powers of the Commissioner also extend to the right to enter and inspect premises where a warrant has been obtained and the Commissioner believes that any of the data protection principles have been or are being contravened. Warrants may be issued by a circuit judge who must be satisfied that there are reasonable grounds for suspecting that an offence has been or is being committed.

To enforce compliance with the data protection principles, the Commissioner can serve three types of notice. They are as follows.

Enforcement notice

This requires the data user to take specified action to comply with the particular principle. Failure to comply with the notice is a criminal offence. In deciding whether to serve an enforcement notice, the Commissioner will need to consider whether the contravention has caused, or is likely to cause, any person damage or distress.

De-registration notice

This cancels the whole or part of a data user's register entry. It would then be a criminal offence for the data user to continue to treat the personal data that is subject to the notice as though it were still registered in the same way.

Transfer prohibition notice

This prevents the data user from transferring personal data overseas if the Commissioner is satisfied that the transfer is likely to lead to a principle being broken. Failure to comply with the notice is a criminal offence.

A data user on whom a notice is served is entitled to appeal against the Commissioner's decision to the Data Protection Tribunal. An appeal against the decision of the Data Protection Tribunal may be made to the High Court in England and Wales or the Court of Session in Scotland.

OFFENCES UNDER THE DPA 1998

- processing without notification

- failure to notify the Commissioner of changes to the notification entry

- processing before expiry of assessable processing time limits or receipt of assessable processing notice within such time (where 'assessable processing' includes, for example, processing likely to cause damage or distress)

- failure to comply with a written request for particulars

- failure to comply with an enforcement/information/special information notice

- knowingly or recklessly making a false statement in compliance with an information notice or special information notice

- intentional obstruction of or failure to give reasonable assistance in execution of a warrant

- unlawful obtaining of personal data

- unlawful selling of personal data

- enforced subject access (see Chapter 3).

NOTIFICATION

The DPA 1984 established a system of registration that was maintained by the Data Protection Registrar. The DPA 1998 introduces a simplified system of notification to replace this. Under part 3 of the DPA 1998, where data is processed using a computer or is recorded with the intention of processing it by means of a computer or the processing is assessable processing (eg likely to cause damage or distress), the data controller has to register the following details ('registerable particulars'):

- name and address

- if a representative has been nominated, the name and address of the representative

- a description of the personal data being/to be processed and of the categories of data subject to which it relates

- a description of the purposes for which the data is being/to be processed

- a description of any recipients to whom the data controller intends to or may wish to disclose the data

- the name or description of any countries or territories outside the EEA to which the data controller transfers or intends to or may wish to transfer the data

- where the personal data is of a type that is exempt from the prohibition and where the notification does not extend to such data, a statement of that fact.

It will be open to any data controller to make a voluntary notification even if it is not statutorily required. One advantage of this is that the data controller will not then be subject to section 24 of the new Act. This requires that, on receipt of a written request from anyone, the data controller must within 21 days make available (free of charge) the same information as would be required under the notification provisions. Failure to comply with section 24 is an offence. If a data controller processes only manual information, he or she will not have to notify but will have to comply with the Act. In terms of notification generally, if a data user has a register entry under the DPA 1984, he or she does not have to notify under the DPA 1998 until the expiry of the existing registry entry or 23 October 2001, whichever is the earlier. The data controller still has to comply with the DPA 1998 and notify the Commissioner of certain changes in processing. Compliance with the DPA 1998 is dependent on whether personal data was being processed before 24 October 1998 (see 'Transitional Provisions' above).

COMPENSATION

If an employee suffers damage as a result of an employer's failure to comply with the provisions of the new Act, the employee may bring a claim of compensation in the High Court or county court that may also include damages for distress. In addition, an order that the employer rectify, block, damage or erase the relevant personal data may also be included in the claim.

6 Future developments

Although the DPA 1998 provides for a period of transitional relief for employers, it is one of the most complex pieces of recent legislation for employers of all sizes to deal with. The aim of the new legislation is to safeguard the right of individuals and the use of personal information relating to them.

Employers will need to carry out an audit of existing procedures and identify existing unofficial channels via which managers and supervisors obtain and provide employee information. Employers should also update or prepare an information policy to fully explain to employees the provisions of and rights granted by the new legislation.

The Data Protection Commissioner has stated that a Code of Practice will be issued that governs the use of personal data by employers. This follows on from a study on the use of personal data in employment undertaken by Robin Chater of the Personnel Policy Research Unit. The Code of Practice will introduce tighter control over the use of employee records in three key areas:

- employee surveillance, involving the collection of data to monitor performance or detect problems, eg interception of e-mail and use of CCTV

- automated processing, eg CV scanning, aptitude and psychometric testing and any means by which employment decisions might be taken automatically

- collection of new and sensitive information, eg genetic tests or results of alcohol or drug testing.

Once the Code of Practice is in place, failure to comply could lead to enforcement action by the Commissioner or a claim for compensation by any individual who has suffered as a result.

The Commissioner will also be responsible for freedom of information issues when the Government's proposals come into force. The Government's key proposals are contained in the Freedom of Information Bill, which establishes a right to information and *applies to public authorities only*. Any person, on making a request to a *public authority* for information, will be entitled to be informed whether that information is held and to have that information communicated to him or her. The Information Commissioner will have the duty to promote good practice and the compliance of public authorities with the Act, to disseminate information and to give advice about the Act. Only some of the data protection principles will apply to personal data held by public authorities. The subject access provisions currently contained in the DPA 1998 will be extended to include unstructured personal data and the notification provisions will be amended so that a public authority will be required to include in its notification to the Commissioner a statement that it is a public authority.

Clearly developments in the control and use of data are not going to cease with the implementation of the DPA 1998. The Human Rights Act 1998, article 8, is also likely to have an impact on the way the DPA 1998 is applied. Article 8 states that everyone has the right to respect for his or her private and family life, home and correspondence. Employers will need to remain both up to date and vigilant to avoid committing offences in relation to the use of individual data.